EAT LIKE A LOCAL- NETHERLANDS

Netherlands Food Guide

Jurgen Shpërdhea

CZYK Publishing Since 2011.

Eat Like a Local

Lock Haven, PA
All rights reserved.
ISBN: 9781698266220

BOOK DESCRIPTION

Are you excited about planning your next trip?

Do you want an edible experience? Would you like some culinary guidance from a local? If you answered yes to any of these questions, then this Eat Like a Local book is for you. Eat Like a Local-Netherlands by author Jurgen Shpërdhea gives you the inside scoop on food in the Netherlands. Culinary tourism is an import aspect of any travel experience. Food has the ability to tell you a story of a destination, its landscapes, and culture on a single plate. Most food guides tell you how to eat like a tourist. Although there is nothing wrong with that, as part of the Eat Like a Local series, this book will give you a food guide from someone who has lived at your next culinary destination.

In these pages, you will discover advice on having a unique edible experience. This book will not tell you exact addresses or hours but instead will give you excitement and knowledge of food and drinks from a local that you may not find in other travel food guides.

Eat like a local. Slow down, stay in one place, and get to know the food, people, and culture. By the time you finish this book, you will be eager and prepared to travel to your next culinary destination.

OUR STORY

Traveling has always been a passion of the creator of the Eat Like a Local book series. During Lisa's travels in Malta, instead of tasting what the city offered, she ate at a large fast-food chain. However, she realized that her traveling experience would have been more fulfilling if she had experienced the best of local cuisines. Most would agree that food is one of the most important aspects of a culture. Through her travels, Lisa learned how much locals had to share with tourists, especially about food. Lisa created the Eat Like a Local book series to help connect people with locals which she discovered is a topic that locals are very passionate about sharing. So please join me and: Eat, drink, and explore like a local.

TABLE OF CONTENTS

DEDICATION

This book is dedicated to my wife Sindy whom I love with all my heart and hope to have my side for eternity.

ABOUT THE AUTHOR

Jurgen Shpërdhea is an Albanian author who lives in the Netherlands for more than five years now. He first got here through his Dutch friend who helped him get settled and now Jurgen is living in South Rotterdam for good. He has learned a lot about the Dutch culture and during this decade he has traveled many places, seen many things and tasted many local foods. It was a bit bizarre at first for him to adapt to the Dutch culinary system but now he got it and he is even able to cook like a local.

HOW TO USE THIS BOOK

    The goal of this book is to help culinary travelers either dream or experience different edible experiences by providing opinions from a local. The author has made suggestions based on their own knowledge. Please do your own research before traveling to the area in case the suggested locations are unavailable.

Travel Advisories: As a first step in planning any trip abroad, check the Travel Advisories for your intended destination.
https://travel.state.gov/content/travel/en/traveladvisories/traveladvisories.html

FROM THE PUBLISHER

Traveling can be one of the most important parts of a person's life. The anticipation and memories that you have are some of the best. As a publisher of the *Eat Like a Local*, Greater Than a Tourist, as well as the popular *50 Things to Know* book series, we strive to help you learn about new places, spark your imagination, and inspire you. Wherever you are and whatever you do I wish you safe, fun, and inspiring travel.

Lisa Rusczyk Ed. D.
CZYK Publishing

Hello. Are you planning to come to the Netherlands soon? Maybe you are coming here on vacation or are planning to stay, but anyhow I bet you would like to know some food tips so that you are prepared of what to do and not to do when you arrive. I have fifty food and travel tips for you that you can follow while being in the Netherlands. If you are coming alone or with family, it doesn't matter. I have all the guidance that you need in Dutch culture. You are going to learn about the place, the restaurants, the people, the food and the culture itself. Don't worry, I promise not to spoil anything interesting that you might want to visit, but I will tell you all about the places you need to visit.

Netherlands

Amsterdam
Netherlands
Climate

	High	Low
January	42	33
February	43	33
March	49	36
April	56	40
May	63	47
June	68	52
July	71	55
August	71	55
September	66	51
October	58	45
November	49	40
December	44	35

GreaterThanaTourist.com

Temperatures are in Fahrenheit degrees.
Source: NOAA

1. RISE & SHINE

Dudok in Het Park – This branch of Dudok is located in a national monument from 1750, in Het Park at the foot of the Euromast. They serve breakfast, coffee with cake, high tea, lunch, and drinks. Foodhallen Rotterdam - This spacious indoor food market, with fifteen local stands, is located in the monumental, robust and characteristic Pakhuismeesteren warehouse.

Bertman's – Bertman's has two locations where you can have an organic, gluten-free and vegan breakfast or lunch. Or you might want to taste something for breakfast as the Chia seed pudding, or perhaps a Japanese savory pancake called Okonomiyaki, for lunch.

Lillith – Head to Lilith for breakfast ranging from American pancakes to eggs benedict or lighter options such as granola and acai.

De Machinist – The menu includes both classical dishes as well as modern dishes. The ingredients are organic and pure.

Osteria Vicini - This place offers a taste of authentic Italian food, serving simple and honest fare. The menu is good, but don't forget to check out the daily specials posted on the wall.

2. FINE DINING

Kino Rotterdam – At Ayla, you'll find yourself at a Spanish marketplace, Arabic bazaar or even in a New York alley. On the constantly changing menu, you'll find tapas with a twist, but always with respect for tradition.

Heroine – Enjoy delicious dishes, tasty wines and a high-level of service. You can choose between a 4, 5 or 7-course dinner. The dishes are simple but made with an eye for special techniques and taste.

Aji – Aji is Spanish for pepper, an important ingredient in the kitchen. The owners, with a passion for South American cuisine, offer an original alternative to popular French cuisine.

Restaurant De Jong – This place is opened from Jim de Jong a chef who loves to use products of the season. Apparently, he also loves farming since he has built his own garden in the kitchen from where he gets all the plants and vegetables. You can choose between a vegetable, meat or fish menu.

3. CASUAL DINING

Supermercado – This cozy place is reminiscent of a bubbling South-American cantina. Enjoy one of the many meat, fish or vegetarian dishes prepared on the charcoal grill.

Deli Bird – Delibird owner Wiland Toelen can be credited for bringing in the Dutch culture a piece of the real Thai culture. The interior is modest, without fancy walls or decor.

De Ballentent - This old fashioned brown port pub is an international place for businessmen, seamen, and dockers. The specialty is the traditional Dutch meatball, which can be found in many varieties on the menu.

Coppi – Coppi serves breakfast, lunch, snacks, and drinks, but is also a place where exclusive, bike-related products are sold. The place is named after famous cyclist Fausto Coppi.

FG Restaurant & FG Food Labs - Michelin-star chef Francois Geurds belongs to the absolute top. The flavors he creates are innovative and unsurpassed. At Station Hofplein you'll find two of his restaurants next to each other. Francois Geurds is the only chef in the Netherlands with a special taste-lab where he

experiments with ingredients and preparation
techniques.

4. PLACES TO EAT WITH A VIEW

Aloha – Aloha is a bar and restaurant located in
the former Tropicana swimming complex. It has a
large area to relax and enjoy a meal while you take a
look at the view from the riverside terrace.

Op Het Dak – Op Het Dak is a unique restaurant
and coffee bar on a roof located in the city center of
Rotterdam. It has a nice view of the DakAkker,
Holland's first rooftop farm, and urban garden.

Ss Rotterdam - On the past cruise liner called the
ss Rotterdam you will find there two restaurants: Lido
and Club Room. The first one an informal restaurant
and the second one a luxurious one where you can
take your family. The Lido has a real Dutch feel but
international cuisine and the terrace of the restaurant
is on the deck showing a view over Rotterdam.

Fenix Food Factory - One of the old Fenix
quayside warehouses houses an indoor market for
fresh foods where you can shop for authentic and
traditional products. To better enjoy the view of

Rotterdam skyline I like to sit on the benches and simply be present at the moment.

5. PICTURES TO TAKE

If you are really passionate about taking pictures and posting them on your social media accounts I would like to suggest to you a few places you can visit where you can take inspiring snapshots. The first place that my wife took a picture was Rotterdam Central Station. There you will find these huge skyscrapers and a beautiful open space to relax. The pictures you can take there are going to be a beautiful memory of the city's center along with the central station. The second place I would advise you to go for a picture is Erasmus Bridge, but you want to go there at night. The view is going to be perfect with the light of the city reflecting on the calm waters of the river and the huge cruise ships that are parked right below the skyscrapers where the headquarters of Port of Rotterdam are positioned. And the final place I would recommend for you to take pictures is South Park. There is this beautiful landscape with random tree groups here and there and the big reservoirs. When the sun sets or rises the view can truly be magical and inspire you deeply. After all, nature is better than anything else as a source of inspiration.

6. WHY VISIT

If you are not sure whether you would like to visit Rotterdam or not I will give you a few reasons why you should visit this city. First of all the culture here is not as much as Dutch as in the other places of the Netherlands. This is because a lot of people from different countries and ethnicities have migrated here and now 60% of Rotterdam's population is foreign. So with all these people you will have the chance to know different cultures in just one city and that can educate you and give you a lot more information than you've had about other cultures. Second of all the infrastructure of the city is really interesting and really easy. If you are in a metro line you will see a map that shows all the stations from North to South, and East to West. I have never been lost in this city during my staying here. And third of all, you want to visit because of the food. There are so many varieties of food that you can try from salty to sweet, to spicy and sour.

7. BEST TIMES TO VISIT

For the best time to visit this city or the Netherlands, in general, I would recommend spring and summer. You don't want to be here during the fall or winter since life can get a little bit too much boring with the unstable weather. The Netherlands are up in the North and the place doesn't get many sunny days during the year, being 100 of them out of 365. It is during the spring and summer that more people go out and they go on vacations or have fun during the night because even the weather allows you to do so. Especially from May to July, the odds of having fun and meeting with new people are much, much higher than the other months. I have tried the winter and fall here and let me tell you it sucks. Constant rain and grey skies and not many people moving in the streets even during the day. This is because these are the periods of work overflow and people don't have much time to party to go out. But during the spring and summer when the sun is out more often, you will see locals having barbecues, young people going out and you will even have the chance to ride the bike more and get around the city.

8. CURRENCY TO CARRY

The normal currency that is used in the Netherlands is euros but I wouldn't recommend having other options with you. I am a freelancer and I get my money via a prepaid Mastercard that functions only in dollars. And the problem with that is that most of the businesses and stores here accept payments via card but it has to be in euros. I cannot remember how many times my card got declined in a grocery store or a restaurant because it is in dollars. And if you pay cash then euros have to be a must. I have tried to pay in cash with dollars and most of the people here don't accept it and it is not so worth it to go up and down for an exchange point. Make sure to have the official Europian currency with you and you'll be fine. Otherwise, you will find yourself struggling like me that I would leave the groceries at a corner of the store whenever my card would get declined and go around looking for an ATM machine and then an exchange point where I would turn the dollars into euros.

9. WHERE TO STAY

If you don't have a local friend like I did that kept me in his house, (that didn't end up so well for me), then the options are you might stay in a hostel. And the options for the hostels are limitless. Depends on what you are looking for and remember that like everything else in life you get what you paid for. If you get a cheap hostel up North, chances are that you are going to get a stop on a bunk bed, in something that looks like a warehouse where other 50 or 100 bunk beds are stored and other people will sleep there too. But with a little bit more money you might get a nicer option. If you are really concerned about privacy, a private room in a hostel wouldn't cost as much as it would if you reserve a room in a normal hotel. And you can choose your room with preferences, like the Love Room if you are a couple, or King Room if you are traveling alone. Then about shared rooms, for a little bit more money you can get into a bunk bed with a maximum three other people inside. So two bunk beds per room and the conditions are going to be way better.

10. HOW FOOD TEACHES ABOUT HISTORY AND CULTURE

Personally, I don't wish to offend the Dutch culture or people but the first time that I tasted traditional Dutch food, (croquettes with mayonnaise or spicy sauce), I thought it was tasteless and cold. Then I wondered if the culture and the people are the same. Fortunately no because I have met bed people, but also really good and caring people. The food can tell you that Dutch people love boiled or roasted food. They simply love it and they like to eat it with too much garlic and spicy sauce. What they like to eat too is too much fat and oil in their food. I was in this barbecue one time and the people there were eating grilled meat, and they gave me a portion which I gladly accepted, but then I saw that the meat was full of oil. The Dutch people like to associate their food with some beer and that is why they prefer greasy food. They don't like things that are really hot and they don't like food that takes a lot of time to cook it. They would rather have a tasteless prepared salad from the supermarket and eat it with some boiled potatoes, then to cook a homemade meal which is going to be more delicious but is going to take much more time.

11. STREET FOOD – WHAT YOU NORMALLY ORDER

Whenever I was hungry and I wanted to go eat something outside I would always go for either KFC or something down the line of eastern fast-food chain restaurants. Other options were unconsiderable for me. I would either take my wife to KFC and have some burgers with chicken wings and potatoes, or I would go by a Turkish fast food near my house, just a couple of blocks away and I would order two shwarma's, one spicy and the other normal. If you are wondering what is a Shwarma, is an eastern food recipe where they take this aluminum container and they put inside salad, vegetables, meat, potatoes, cheese, and other stuff and they would put it all down in layers. Layer after layer they would add everything and on top, they would either put garlic sauce of spicy sauce. Another option that I tried was Vietnamese food from a stand in the street. The old man had fairly cheap prices and he would give you something that looked like a hotdog but would tase as something completely different.

12. FESTIVALS / FOOD / CRAFT FAIRS

The Secret Garden – There's a hidden oasis waiting to be found where you can enjoy music, food workshops and art in the city center.

In the Grip of Winter fest – Expect heavy metal, death metal and more. The headliner of the festival is October tide. Location in Baroeg.

NN Marathon Rotterdam – The world's top athletes and thousands of runners get to experience what it is like to finish the renowned Coolsingel in the city center.

Kralingse Bos Festival – King's Day festival with performances from techno to hip hop, including Chris Liebing and Craig David. Location at Kralingse Bos.

Oranjebitter – An exuberant orange party on the King's Day with hip hop, house, disco, and fun games. Location at Het Park.

Circus X Festival – A festival with tasty hits, funny performances, a lot of craziness and amazing shows. Location at Oranjepolder Hoek van Holland

Rotterdam Rooftop Days – Over 40 roofs are open to the public for exciting discoveries, informal drinks, intimate concerts, silent discos, and film nights and sports activities.

RYPP Wine Festival – Delicious wines, culinary delights, intimate musical performances, DJ's and a silent disco.

13. PORT & BEACH

Spido - Go on a tour with Spido, one of Rotterdam's biggest attractions. The Port of Rotterdam tour is about 75 minutes and you'll experience sails year-round which will give you a short but powerful impression of Rotterdam's container ports.

Maeslantkering – The Maeslant Storm Surge Barrier is the largest movable flood barrier in the world and protects the area against flooding. Visit the Keringhuis information center for an impression of the barrier.

FutureLand – A visit to the free FutureLand Information Center will not only tell you everything you need to know about the developing port, at Maasvlakte 2 you will see the biggest container ships and the most modern container terminals with your own eyes.

Rotterdam Beach – Sea, beach, promenade, harbor, polders, and attractions: Hoek van Holland is very versatile. In the summer it's a pleasant, bustling seaside resort but Hoek van Holland is also attractive to visit in the other seasons with a great cultural offering, a diverse hinterland, and giant ships from the international Port of Rotterdam passing by.

14. DRINKS & BITES

Kaapse Maria - Discover surprising and creative dishes that are ideal for combining with the craft beer from the Kaapse Brouwers. With 24 beers on tap, there is plenty of choices.

Brasserie Schielandshuis – The menu focuses on Rotterdam cuisine: honest, no-nonsense and with local products. Stop by for coffee, lunch or a drink.

Thoms Stadsbrouwerij – Between the brewhouse, self-serve tables and at the longest bar in Rotterdam you can enjoy one of the home-brewed beers. The beers are unpasteurized and unfiltered to deliver a unique taste experience.

Brouwerij Noordt – This brewery is found in the imposing building on the former Roteb site along the Rotte. Nothing could be more Rotterdam. A beer tank is tapped every Friday and everyone in the tasting room can test the new brew.

De Gele Kanarie – De Gele Kanarie serves lunch, dinner and various types of beer, wine, and mixed drinks. They also have their own brewed beer on tap: DGK or De Gele Kanarie (Yellow Canary).

15. SWEET CRAVINGS

Urban Bakery – Urban Bakery is the place to go for the freshly baked bread, cakes, and other pastries. The recipes are inspired by international cuisines and what comes out of the oven is determined by the fruits of the season.

Lof der Zoetheid – Anastasia & Elena de Ruyter are mother and daughter with Russian roots. Elena's specialty is pastry, Anastasia cooks and is a designer. Don't miss the afternoon tea with biological bread, scones, and pastries.

Koskela – Koskela is one of the local favorites in Rotterdam. In this store, you will find freshly baked cookies, muffins, scones, and cakes.

Baker's Dough

This is the place to eat fresh and safe cookie dough. Feel at home in the large kitchen and create your favorite dough in 3 simple and quick steps with various toppings.

Sharp Sharp

100% vegan cake bar where they serve various cookies, cakes, and juices. All their products are entirely plant-based, made without animal products and are also gluten and refined sugar-free.

16. SOUVENIR FOOD

If you wish to try some souvenir food then you should go to a market place. Why? Because they have everything there, from fresh vegetables to open cooked food and servers are really polite. You can try some Vietnamese food or some traditional fish. You will find these places in the streets, like stands with the prices listed all outside and the taste of the food is going to be delicious.

17. PLACES TO SHOP

De Bijenkorf – As busy as the beehive De Bijenkorf is named after, this trendy department store always has new products and international brands in fashion, cosmetics, accessories, home decoration and more. Hema – No department store could be as fundamentally Dutch as the HEMA. It's the most famous products is indisputably the juicy smoked sausage.

Hudson's Bay – This department store not only offers a lot of fashion, cosmetics, and interior accessories but also toys, books and La Place restaurant. Topshop and Saks OFF 5th can be found in the same building.

Donner – It's easy to lose track of time in a bookshop this size, browsing through art books, novels, magazines, cookbooks, travel guides, and comic books.

Funkie House – With a collection featuring over sixty clothing brands, plus an equally varied clientele, Funkie House can justifiably call itself a home to both men and women who are into street fashion.

Bohemian by Jibodh – Whether you are looking for masculine and cool, stylish and classic, or vintage and timeless, the Jibodh brothers are happy to help you find the right outfit.

18. DRESS CODE

The dressing code is something out of a novel in the Netherlands. The style of the people is so emo or dark and you have people dressing like that everywhere. Girls wear dark makeup and they wear brown or black clothes mostly. Maybe it has something to do with the North. One thing that I don't see in the Netherlands is girls wearing shorts or skirts. I can surely say I have never seen a girl in the Netherlands dress like that and it must be something that has to do with the dressing code. I have a confession to make. My wife would wear shorts or skirts since its normal for girls to dress like that in Albania, and I would have a problem each time I would go out with her. People, especially drunk men, would look at her and turn their heads as they have never seen a woman before and this would get me so jealous, even though my wife would joke about it. If you are planning to visit alone or with a partner, the dressing code is one of the main things you should respect. You cannot go around wearing a black hoodie with your face all covered and headphones in your ears, they will think that you are going to rob them or something. Keep it simple, stick to the jeans and long or short sleeves shirts and you will be just fine.

19. SOMETHING NEW OR SHOCKING TO TRAVELERS

Something new or surprising that travelers might find while they are staying here is the number of bikes there are in the Netherlands. There are just too much of them and there is, in fact, a rumor that in the Netherlands there are more bikes than people. I don't know if this rumor is true, however I see people riding the bike everywhere. And you have to be careful because they don't go slow, especially when they are out in groups. If you are riding the bike in the red lane and you hear people ringing behind you, it is a sign that you must either go faster than you already are, or you must get out of the way because they will crush with you. I know it sounds a bit exaggerated but I am not kidding you. It has happened to me multiple times. But surely what is one of the most surprising things is people giving away their bike to you for free. This also happens a lot and don't be surprised when it happens to you. Maybe the bike has a minor problem or maybe they are getting a new one, for whatever reason, strangers might approach you sometimes and give you away their bike for completely free. Someone actually gave me a bike a week ago and it has been going great so far.

20. WHO TO CONTACT FOR HELP

Among looking at the city and going around the town to enjoy the food and the view, I have had a couple of unpleasant instances where I had to call for help. I had to be creative sometimes, other times I just had to deal with my paranoia and suppress my deepest fears. The Netherlands is a beautiful country and there are many things to enjoy here, but you also know that cannabis is legal here. I have had problems with cannabis this year. I have been a smoker for five years and this is the first years that I have had these deep paranoia problems whenever I get high. They are so bad in fact that I have called the ambulance a couple of times, saying that I am having a heart attack. It was only a panic attack. If you are in an emergency, for example you fell off a bike and broke something, or you got involved in a car accident, 911 is the first number you should call. They speak fluent English. They will ask for which department you wish to be connected and the location. Then they will ask you about what happened and after a couple of questions help will be on the way. Be careful. If you don't have insurance, healthcare prices can get pretty expensive in this country. So stay safe and try to avoid getting in any trouble. 911 works for the police, the ambulance, and the fire department. No matter the case you can dial it and wait for the help to come. During my weed paranoia, the ambulance came for about 15 minutes. 15 longest minutes of my life. But thank God I made it out alive and promised to myself not to ever smoke again.

21. LEARN SOME PHRASES

Now let's become a little bit Dutch by learning some of the most basic phrases. You will need these phrases when you are since Dutch people prefer to speak their own language instead of the English language. So you say 'hoy' or 'doo-ee' for 'hi' and you write them 'hoi' and 'doei'. You write 'ja' for 'yes' but you pronounce it as 'yah' and write 'nee' for 'no' but you pronounce it as 'nay'. If you want to buy something and you want to ask for the price you say 'vat kohst ut' and you write it as 'wat kost het?' which means 'how much is it?' After you take what you bought and you want to say 'thank you' you say 'dahnk ew vehl', which is written as 'dank u wel', and the shopkeeper will probably respond with 'khrahkh khuh dahn' which is written as 'graag gedaan' and means 'you're welcome'.

22. WHERE TO BUY AND NOT BUY SOME GROCERIES

If you like cooking indoors then you want to buy some groceries and now I am about to tell you the best place where you can buy and not buy some groceries for yourself or your family. If you are on the South Side of Rotterdam then the place you want to go for Groceries is Dirk. This is a supermarket where you can find some cheap and high-quality groceries for you. The prices are affordable and the food is good. And on top of everything you can fill in your fridge with very little money. If you want fresh vegetables and fruits you might want to check out Afrikaanderplein. A street market is held every Wednesday where you can find fresh vegetables and fruits and the sellers are all so polite and quite funny. Now on the downside, I will tell you where not to buy groceries in the Netherlands. Small grocery stores run by different races. The food there will be mostly expired, cheap and not edible. Careful and always check for the expiration date. I went into a grocery store one day and got me a Pepsi and a candy bar. When I walked out I checked the expiration date on the Pepsi and it had expired a month ago. I walked in again to complain and the seller told me to grab another one. When I checked on the fridge,

23. REMEMBER TO BRING THESE ITEMS WITH YOU

What items you would need to bring with you? Definitely an umbrella. When I first came to the Netherlands I had no umbrella with me and I thought I wouldn't need one since it was summer when I came here. But I was so wrong. It can start raining anytime and it is nearly unpredictable. One time the sun is out and it's hot, the next the wind can blow like crazy and another time rain might start out of nowhere. So you will need an umbrella if you are planning to go out. Another item you will need is a sachel to keep your personal belongings, such as your passports, cellphone, wallet, keys and other stuff. Since you are not local here and you don't have a Dutch ID you will need more than a wallet for verification if the police stop you, so a sachel is a perfect item you want to use. I still have the same sachel for five years now and it has been so handy with all the movements around. I never lose anything from it and more importantly, I never lose it out of sight since it is always on my shoulder and waist.

24. STAY SAFE

You want to stay safe here, then never cross the road without assuring that there are no cars. People here drive a bit too much like crazy and the week that I came here I saw a car accident. I haven't seen one in my country for years, and soon as I came here I saw one. Happens for a reason. People don't usually break the street rules but they drive pretty damn fast even in the small roads inside the neighborhoods. My wife is used to crossing the road seconds before the light turns green and she has been nearly hit multiple times. Another thing about staying safe is to never go out alone after midnight, especially on dark allies and if you are thinking of going to a small night nature trip, it is a big no-no. the kind of people that are around are not so friendly and I am talking about crackheads, drunk people or people with anger issues that will taunt you for no reason at all. So you want to stay safe. Go out in a group or stay inside during the night.

25. APPS TO DOWNLOAD BEFORE YOU COME TO THE NETHERLANDS

Maritime Museum App – This app is a digital experience, full of video clips and digital souvenirs. Including an audio tour of the museum and the harbor. You can get it for free on Google Play or App Store.

Rotterdam Tourist App – This is a perfect app for you who love real-time experiences. Here you will find many guidelines about restaurants, coffee bars, sweet shops, and many other things. You can download this app simply by searching for it on Google Play or on the App Store. This app is a must-have.

9292 – While it sounds like a mathematical riddle, this app actually is crucial for you to download before you leave. It is full of directions and guidelines on how and where to travel. It shows you the precise hours of the metro lines, buses, trams and other methods of transportation and also how to get there. It is free and doesn't take up much space from your phone. Find it on the App Store or Google Play.

Thuisbezorgd.nl – How would you like to have all the pizzerias, fast foods, restaurants and eating places all packed in one app? Well before you step foot in the Netherlands, this app will save your stomach as it lets you order food in real-time, with very flexible gadgets on the menus and real-time tracking on your food. Definitely must have this app.

26. ALCOHOLIC DRINKS

As far as alcoholic drinks Dutch people love to drink beer most of all. They love different kinds of beer from black to light, and they love to drink it while eating some fresh barbecue meat or some snacks. They love drinking their beer with almost anything, especially with some cannabis. That is their favorite. But you will have other options for alcohol. If you are a wine lover you can find wine for a really cheap price in the supermarkets or even in bars. If you prefer whiskey or something like whiskey then you can again either go in the supermarkets or a bar. The prices are different and logically the supermarket has cheaper prices but if you don't want to drink at home but rather outside, then a bar is the perfect solution for you. I have stayed home with people and they wouldn't go out as much. Instead they would just sit in the room and drink some wine there. However I have lived with other people who would almost never come in the house and they were always outside drinking in bars and hanging out for their own fun. So for the alcoholic drinks, the options are in many and you can choose what you really like to do or where you really like to drink and what.

27. A DRAMATIC MEMORY

I was staying at this shared house with my wife, where there were two other guys living in there. One of them was constantly hitting on my wife but I was unaware of it at the time. One day she and I had a fight and this guy, (who happened to also be the landlord), heard us and came in the room. She was crying so he took me out of the room and talked to her in private. All in all he told me that she didn't want me in the house anymore so he kicked me out. She called me half an hour later saying that she had kissed him and that she was truly sorry and that she wanted to meet with me. We met, found another place and ever since then I have been trying to forgive her. Careful. Don't live in a shared house if you are in a couple.

28. WHAT DOES THIS PLACE TEACH YOU ABOUT YOURSELF?

What this place has taught me about myself is that I am strong and I can endure. Ever since I have been here I have been scammed multiple times by people. I have been kicked out of the house multiple times. I have been arrested once, for passport verification, (it turned out it wasn't fake and they let me go). Through all hell and high water, I have survived and I have become a better human being. The thing about the Netherlands and especially Rotterdam, it teaches you that you can belong anywhere you want to belong and it is all about the frame of mind. It is all about loving what you already have. This is because as I said, 60% of Rotterdam's population are emigrants, and meeting with different people that all speak and act the same from the fact that they have lived there for many years now, has taught me this

about myself. I have learned how to love
stronger and forgive more than ever before,
because the challenges that I have faced here, I
have never faced them before in another
country, not even in my own.

29. MUSIC SCENE

Now I am about to drown you in a variety of bands
and events of music that happen here and you will
have so many choices that you won't know where to
go first:

Bands like D'Angelo, Raphael Saadiq, and Snarky
Puppy all gather together to play at Club Doyle for
The Soulful Congregation.

If you love electro music then IPSO will bring up
the house to the o-zone with his skills, playing at
Kolsch, Annabel.

At Bird Rotterdam you will find live music and
after-parties while having long tables where you can
chill with your friends as you have a soul food
experience.

You probably know Oliver Heldens from his hit
Gecko and since then he has been returning to his
homeland to give awesome performances.

30. YOUR NORMAL FOOD CHOICES

My normal food choice while in the Netherlands would be something like fried potatoes with crispy chicken and spicy sauce. I would always have this for lunch and then drink a soda afterward. As for breakfast, I would always have either coffee with some cookies, or cornflakes and milk with honey. I am talking about my normal food choices and what I would personally have on a regular basis. It is not so different from what someone else might have in America. What I would advise for most of you reading this book is to eat inside. Meaning homemade food. You don't want to spend a lot of money by eating outside at different restaurants when you can simply do some groceries and cook inside and not only save money but also create a bit of a routine in your life. Trust me, you will need the routine when you go to another country.

31. DAILY ROUTINE

When it comes to the daily routine, let me tell you that it is a must. For me it was the only way to survive in the Netherlands. You cannot go anywhere without a daily routine. Every time my circumstances changed, my daily routine would change with them. It was imposed on my brain as a survival instinct. When I first got here my life was all a mess. I was staying with this friend who would play games all night long and I started becoming like him. I would sleep at 4 am and then wake up at 1 pm. First of all that is really unhealthy as it can affect your body and mind in a really drastic way. Second of all it would mess up my whole day. I started missing deadlines, not paying attention to work and it all became too overwhelming for me. So in order for me to get back on the track, I had to set a daily routine and stick to it with a sick discipline. And every time my circumstances would change, for example when I got kicked out, I had to change my daily routine to adapt to the new environment that I was in. The point I am trying to make is that you need a daily routine to cope with all the different activities that are going to happen in your life.

32. COFFEE BARS

I am used in my country to go out and have a coffee at a coffee bar sometimes. I like sitting down outside with a coffee mug in front of me smoking a cigarette. It is really relaxing. I have been trying to do the same in the Netherlands but it was bit hard at first until I had to find the right couple of coffee bars. Once used to the routine I would go there regularly every morning to get my dosage of caffeine. You have a couple of options for coffee bars, from Starbucks that is usually near the center or some other coffee bar near the place where you live. You just have to do a bit of research on them.

33. RIDING THE BIKE

Be careful, they might run you over. Almost everyone rides a bike in the Netherlands. People like cycling way more than driving a car. And it is overwhelming sometimes. If you are a slow biker then get out of the way or they will run you over. Stay in your lane and never wear headphones while riding the bike, or you might miss someone ringing the bell behind you, asking you to move. They like to go out in groups and sometimes the bike traffic is worse than the cars traffic. Just be extra careful when you are crossing the street and during the rush hours. You can rent a bike but I would advise buying one since they are really cheap and don't cost that much. Have fun.

34. SAUCES

Dutch people love adding sauces to almost anything. They love their burger with barbecue and spicy sauce on top. They love and I mean completely love garlic sauce. If you got to the grocery store you have an aisle especially for sauces where you have all kinds of flavors and tastes and for different purposes. You have a sauce for sandwiches, a sauce for bread, a sauce for meat and sausages, a sauce for potatoes. I sometimes think that they have a sauce for everything here.

35. AMOUNT OF TIME NEEDED.

Fast foods are really fast. Restaurants not that much but if you are eating like a normal person you might wait a maximum of 15 to 20 minutes for the order to be ready. If you decide to takeout food then your order might take up to 30 minutes depending on what you have ordered but almost everything doesn't surpass half an hour of waiting time as the food doesn't take much time to prepare. Even when I would live with my friend and his mother, she would make us lunch in 15 minutes.

36. NONALCOHOLIC DRINKS

Do you like energy drinks? How about a nice fruit juice? Well these are the most common nonalcoholic drinks in the Netherlands. A smoothie or a Monster energy drink is preferable when you are going out and deciding to feel sober. They also have this kind of colored water, that comes in different tastes and is really good. Though Dutch people have a name for drinking alcohol, (which is true, people here drink a lot), you also have nonalcoholic options you might want to try. You can even drink 0% alcohol beer while you are out at a bar so the choice is really yours.

37. INGREDIENTS

About the most used ingredients, I would include cheese, potatoes, meat, vegetables like peppers and tomatoes, salt, bread, etc. There is a huge list of options for ingredients, for either fast food or restaurants or home-made food and each one of them can be combined in such a way to prepare a perfect meal for yourself or your family. Milk is commonly used with flour and eggs to make home-made cookies with dark chocolate, (which I shall not forget to say that it is exquisite).

38. COFFEE SHOPS

I am going to suggest you only a few coffee shops where I used to go and what I think is trustworthy and then you can find the rest on Maps. The first one is New York coffee shop and is located on the southside of Rotterdam, near the Erasmus bridge. The prices are affordable, the weed is good and basically the place has a hospitality of its own. The other ones you will find them on Witte De With Straat which is one of the most frequented streets of Rotterdam. You will also find bars and fast food there since the street is near the center of the city. The prices can vary and of course are higher than when you go outside the center, but the weed is fairly good along with the options that are more diverse. You can get a brownie or even truffles there and you can party all night long. Don't sleep on the streets, because it's illegal.

39. NIGHT FOOD

There is a bit of a problem to find food during the night in the Netherlands because most of the restaurants close around midnight and anything open after that time would mostly be fast foods or maybe a 24 hours open restaurant. Do your research but don't go too far to eat. A cab can be expensive at night and if you just left the club, tipsy and feeling hungry, take out food would be your best option. Open Google, search for an open fast food or takeout food in the city, place your order and voila, food is on the way.

40. BIRTHDAY DINNERS

All in all I have been on two birthday dinners and let me tell you they are pretty cool. The first one was organized at a karaoke club up North. It was my friend's birthday and his mom had invited his grandfather, a couple of his friends and me. We sang a couple of songs, everyone in the club sang happy birthday to my friend, we had some cake and smoked some weed and that's it. We had a good familiar time and it was just a normal birthday as you might celebrate it everywhere. The second time it was a barbecue birthday. A lady invited us to her backyard as a friend of her had their birthday. We ate grilled meat, drank beer, smoked weed and had a good time while listening to the old people sharing stories around the table.

41. SHARING A HOUSE

I have shared a house three times while in the Netherlands and I can tell you from personal experience this might not be something you might want to do, especially when you don't know the people you are sharing a house with. I am going to tell you what happened to me to the last place that I shared with someone so you can form an idea of what might happen. I was living in a room with my wife and we were in total five people in the house. I and my wife had a room, the landlord had his own room, another guy had a room upstairs and a girl was living up in the attic. People sometimes can be shameless and might try to through dirt on you simply because they don't know you and they want to profit. For example, when we first arrived at the house the sink in the kitchen was blocked and the water wouldn't go down. I opened it the next day and cleaned it up but the problem didn't go away. I told the landlord that I tried to fix the sink and after a few days he and the other guy blamed me for 'breaking' the sink, (it was already blocked when I first entered the house), so according to them, I had to fix it back. Please avoid unpleasant situations like this and better get a room for yourself.

42. SWEETS

I haven't really tried any particular sweets while in the Netherlands though there are a few good options that I might suggest to you. One of them is dough sweets that you might get in a local bakery. They cost very little and are delicious. I would usually go for doughnuts since they are really good and fairly cheap. You can get yourself doughnuts in different flavors in a regular grocery store. Be sure to not sugar overload while you get sweets. Supermarkets have many

options from sweet bread to cakes so you can take
your pick.

43. APPS

About apps that you should have in your
smartphone when you are in the Netherlands, I can
mention a few that are essential for living here. Maps,
which is logical of having since you are in another
country and you need an app to move around and
know where things are located and more importantly,
where you are located. You will need Marktplaast,
which is a great app where you can find anything to
anything. The app has the English option and is very
useful, when you are looking to buy something, like a
mattress if you are planning to stay for a few months
or you can use the app to even rent a house.

44. TAKE OUT

Take out food has a lot of options depending
on what you are looking to order. You can order
a pizza or a full meal of meat and potatoes. You
can order fish and rice along with a bottle of wine
to enjoy if you are in a couple. The order doesn't

take much to arrive and the quality of the food is mostly good if you order to places that have a high rating. Careful though, if you think on being cheap while you are placing your order to a place with bad reviews but cheap prices then you are going to get what you pay.

45. RESERVATIONS

For places that ask for a reservation I would advise to book a few days or a week in advance because chances are that you won't find a spot. For example, if you go at Loetje, a place in Rotterdam where they serve beef, you have to make a reservation at least ten days before since they are always full and if you make a reservation later than that then you will end up with a not so great of a spot. So if you are looking to enjoy the food and the view at the same time, I would advise going to their website and making a reservation beforehand and paying with your credit card.

46. STREET ART

The Netherlands is filled with street artists who leave their mark on different places of a city. For example, in Rotterdam I had the chance to street perform with a guy who would do beatboxing and it was a really amazing experience. But apart from music I would see street sculptures that you would mostly find them in parks. Graffiti is common too and in some neighborhoods, you have walls painted with different pictures and messages. I once got a picture form a street painter who would do beautiful portraits within seconds. And it was cheap for what I got in return.

47. COMMON EXPRESSIONS

When you walk in the streets of the Netherlands, sometimes you would hear people talk half English, (mostly curse words) and it makes you wonder if their language is connected to English. The first word that I learned while in the Netherlands was Weltrusten, which means 'sleep tight' and it is only used when someone is going to sleep, (though at first, I would use it as to say 'goodnight', which was the wrong use). Commonly as American people use the expression 'yeah man' when answering a yes or no question, Dutch people say 'yah man' and you will hear this a lot.

48. HOMEGROWN FOOD

I'll be honest with you, the only homegrown food that I ever tried so far are the common vegetables like tomatoes and cucumbers. Much better taste than the ones you buy at the grocery store that basically taste like plastic. I tasted homegrown food for the first time at a place I was staying in. The building had three stores and I was living on the last floor. I had the view from behind the building and I could see that behind my building there was a nice organized garden with vegetables and small animals, like a couple of chickens and rabbits. The landlord knew who the neighbors were so he politely asked them for some homegrown tomatoes, cucumbers, and peppers and they were so kind as to give us that for free. My wife cooked for me and she prepared a delicious meal, (one of the best meals I've had while in the Netherlands), and it was all made with homegrown food, except the chicken breast that we took from the grocery store. That's it as far as my experiences with homegrown food.

49. TAKE OUT AND DINE IN

About take out food the procedure you have to go through is not complicated at all. There are actually many applications online where you can order food and have it right at your doorstep. You can either decide to pay cash or by credit card and that is really up to you. The options are really limitless since you can order pizza or Turkish food, Chinese, how about some Indian food, it is really up to you. One thing you have to know though, the delivery guy won't always come up to give you the order and sometimes you have to go down, (in case you live on an upper floor) to get it, even if the building has an elevator. And make sure that they have included everything you ordered. Once time that I ordered Shwarma for myself and my wife, the delivery guy forgot to bring the garlic cause which wasn't that pleasant because it would make our meal ten times more delicious. I couldn't complain about it since I only saw that the sauce was missing when I came upstairs, (he didn't come up to deliver the food), and the delivery guy had already gone. Complaining to the application seemed completely irrational so I just let it go. You better check everything while you are there with the delivery guy.

50. SUPPORTING LOCALS

Ever since the first days that I came to the Netherlands, I had the opportunity to help locals with various house chores. The very first week that I was here, my friend and I went to this old lady's house to help her get rid of a carpet that she hadn't moved nor cleaned for thirty years ever since her son passed away in that room. It was a great and hard experience but at least I had the chance to support a local. Another time we went to one of his neighbors and helped her with some heavy things in the back yard and in return she invited us on a barbecue she was holding that weekend. It was the first time for me to do this in a different country and it felt really good while I was doing something for someone else and enjoying some local food in return.

READ OTHER BOOKS BY CZYK PUBLISHING

Greater Than a Tourist- St. Croix US Birgin Islands USA: 50 Travel Tips from a Local by Tracy Birdsall

Greater Than a Tourist- Toulouse France: 50 Travel Tips from a Local by Alix Barnaud

Children's Book: *Charlie the Cavalier Travels the World* by Lisa Rusczyk

Eat Like a Local

Follow *Eat Like a Local on* Amazon.

Made in United States
North Haven, CT
23 July 2022

21736050R00043